Contents

Introduction

The book "The Ten Titans in Psychology and Psychoanalysis" is dedicated to ten of the most notable scientists in the world of psychology and psychoanalysis, namely Sigmund Freud, Carl Gustav Jung, Alfred Adler, Karen Horney, Viktor Frankl, Erik Berne, Carl Rodgers, Abraham Maslow, Erich Fromm, Ivan Pavlov. In it, you will find some of the Big Ten's most inspiring, interesting, intriguing and popular thoughts and reflections. The book is a valuable friend of every lover of psychology and psychoanalysis and a faithful assistant to every clinical specialist, consultant, and psychologist. It covers a wide range of questions about the clinical practice, philosophy, and life of these ten eminent scientists. With this book, you will not only read the words of one author about another, but you will have the opportunity to become familiar with the words of the experts themselves. This, in turn, will help you get to know their thoughts, feelings, and philosophy about life, work, religion, man, relationships, mental illness and suffering, and more. I wish everyone a pleasant minute of reading this humble but interesting book. Have a nice and successful day! Best regards, Valentin Boyadzhiev!

About the author

Valentin Boyadzhiev is a trained nutritionist, graduated Master of Psychology in "Psychology and Psychopathology of Development". He has acquired Professional Qualification "Teacher of Psychology" and Postgraduate Professional Qualification "Psychological Counseling in Psychosomatic and Social Adaptation Disorders". He has obtained a Psychoanalysis Diploma and he is currently specializing in Psychoanalytic Psychotherapy. He is a member of the Association "Bulgarian Psychoanalytic Space", "International Society of Applied Psychoanalysis" and „International Alliance of Holistic Therapists". He is a lecturer on issues related to nutrition, diet, supplementation, food and sports. He is also a teacher and a lecturer in the field of psychology, logic, ethics, law, and

philosophy. He has been a school psychologist since 2017. He has been participating annually in scientific conferences on psychology, psychotherapy, dietetics and medicine. His main interest and practice are in the field of psychoanalysis and clinical psychology.

Sigmund Freud Quotes

A civilization which leaves so large a number of its participants unsatisfied and drives them into revolt neither has nor deserves the prospect of a lasting existence.A love that does not discriminate seems to me to forfeit a part of its own value, by doing an injustice to its object; and secondly, not all men are worthy of love.

Ψ

A man should not strive to eliminate his complexes but to get into accord with them: they are legitimately what directs his conduct in the world. A man who has been the indisputable favorite of his mother keeps for life the feeling of a conqueror.

Ψ

A piece of creative writing, like a day-dream, is a continuation of, and a substitute for, what was once the play of childhood.

Ψ

A religion, even if it calls itself a religion of love, must be hard and unloving to those who do not belong to it.

Ψ

A transference neurosis corresponds to a conflict between ego and id, a narcissistic neurosis corresponds to that between ego and super-ego, and psychosis to that between ego and outer world.

Ψ

A woman should soften but not weaken a man.

Ψ

America is a mistake, a giant mistake.

Ψ

America is the most grandiose experiment the world has seen, but, I am afraid, it is not going to be a success.

Ψ

Anatomy is destiny.

Ψ

Beauty has no obvious use; nor is there any clear cultural necessity for it. Yet civilization could not do without it.

Ψ

Before you diagnose yourself with depression or low self-esteem, first make sure that you are not, in fact, just surrounded by unpleasant people. Being entirely honest with oneself is a good exercise.

Ψ

Children are completely egoistic; they feel their needs intensely and strive ruthlessly to satisfy them. Civilization began the first time an angry person cast a word instead of a rock.

Ψ

Civilized society is perpetually menaced with disintegration through this primary hostility of men towards one another.

Ψ

Conscience is the internal perception of the rejection of a particular wish operating within us.

Ψ

Conservatism is too often a welcome excuse for lazy minds, loath to adapt themselves to fast changing conditions. Dreams are often most profound when they seem the most crazy.

Ψ

Children are completely egoistic; they feel their needs intensely and strive ruthlessly to satisfy them.

Ψ

Dreams are the royal road to the unconscious.

Ψ

Everyone owes nature a death. Everywhere I go I find a poet has been there before me.

Ψ

Experience teaches that for most people there is a limit beyond which their constitution cannot comply with the demands of civilization. All who wish to reach a higher standard than their constitution will allow, fall victims to neurosis. It would have been better for them if they could have remained less "perfect". From error to error, one discovers the entire truth.

Ψ

He does not believe that does not live according to his belief. He that has eyes to see and ears to hear may convince himself that no mortal can keep a secret. If his lips are silent, he chatters with his fingertips; betrayal oozes out of him at every pore. He who knows how to wait for need make no concessions.

Ψ

How bold one gets when one is sure of being loved.

Ψ

Human beings are funny. They long to be with the person they love but refuse to admit openly. Some are afraid to show even the slightest sign of affection because of fear. Fear that their feelings may not be recognized, or even worst, returned. But one thing about human beings puzzles me the most is their conscious effort to be connected with the object of their affection even if it kills them slowly within.

Ψ

Humanity has in the course of time had to endure from the hands of science two great outrages upon its naive self-love. The first was when it realized that our earth was not the center of the universe, but only a tiny speck in a world-system of a magnitude hardly conceivable; this is associated in our minds with the name of Copernicus, although Alexandrian doctrines taught something very similar. The second was when biological research robbed man of his peculiar privilege of having been specially created, and relegated him to a descent from the animal world, implying an ineradicable animal nature in him: this transvaluation has been accomplished in our own time upon the instigation of Charles Darwin, Wallace, and their predecessors, and not without the most violent opposition from their contemporaries. But man's craving for grandiosity is now suffering the third and most bitter blow from present-day psychological research which is endeavoring to

11

prove to the ego of each one of us that he is not even master in his own house, but that he must remain content with the veriest scraps of information about what is going on unconsciously in his own mind. We psycho-analysts were neither the first nor the only ones to propose to mankind that they should look inward, but it appears to be our lot to advocate it most insistently and to support it by empirical evidence which touches every man closely.

Ψ

I became aware of my destiny: to belong to the critical minority as opposed to the unquestioning majority.

Ψ

I cannot think of any need in childhood as strong as the need for a father's protection.
I never want to belong to any club that would have someone like me as a member. If children could if adults knew.

Ψ

If you don't like a person it's because they remind you of something you don't like about yourself. If youth knew; if age could. Illusions commend themselves to us because they save us pain and allow us to enjoy pleasure instead. We must, therefore, accept it without complaint when they sometimes collide with a bit of reality against which they are dashed to pieces. Immorality, no less than morality, has at all times found support in religion.

Ψ

In matters of sexuality we are at present, every one of us, ill or well, nothing but hypocrites.

Ψ

In mourning it is the world which has become poor and empty; in melancholia, it is the ego itself. In the depths of my heart, I can't help being convinced that my dear fellow-men, with a few exceptions, are worthless. In the small matters trust the mind, in the large ones the heart.

Ψ

The instinct of love toward an object demands a mastery to obtain it, and if a person feels they can't control the object or feel threatened by it, they act negatively toward it.
It goes without saying that a civilization which leaves so large a number of its participants

unsatisfied and drives them into revolt neither has nor deserves the prospect of a lasting existence.

Ψ

It is a predisposition of human nature to consider an unpleasant idea untrue, and then it is easy to find arguments against it.

Ψ

It is impossible to escape the impression that people commonly use false standards of measurement — that they seek power, success and wealth for themselves and admire them in others, and that they underestimate what is of true value in life.

Ψ

It is impossible to overlook the extent to which civilization is built up upon a renunciation of instinct.

Ψ

It is not attention that the child is seeking, but love.

Ψ

It would be very nice if there were a God who created the world and was a benevolent providence, and if there were a moral order in the universe and an after-life, but it is a very striking fact that all this is exactly as we are bound to wish it to be.

Ψ

Life, as we find it, is too hard for us; it brings us too many pains, disappointments, and impossible tasks. In order to bear it, we cannot dispense with palliative measures… There are perhaps three such measures: powerful deflections, which cause us to make light of our misery; substitutive satisfactions, which diminish it; and intoxicating substances, which make us insensible to it.

Ψ

Love and work are the cornerstones of our humanness.

Ψ

Love in the form of longing and deprivation lowers the self regard.

Ψ

Man has, as it were, become a kind of prosthetic God.

Ψ

*Maturity is the ability to postpone gratification.
Men are more moral than they think and far more
immoral than they can imagine.
The liberty of the individual is no gift of
civilization. It was greatest before there was any
civilization.*

Ψ

*Men are strong so long as they represent a strong
idea.*

Ψ

*Most people do not really want freedom, because
freedom involves responsibility, and most people
are frightened of responsibility.*

Ψ

*My love is something valuable to me which I
ought not to throw away without reflection.
Neurosis is no excuse for bad manners. Neurosis
is the inability to tolerate ambiguity.*

Ψ

*Neurotics complain of their illness, but they make
the most of it, and when it comes to taking it away
from them they will defend it like a lioness her
young.*

No neurotic harbors thoughts of suicide which are not murderous impulses against others redirected upon himself.

Ψ

No, our science is no illusion. But an illusion it would be to suppose that what science cannot give us we can get elsewhere.

Ψ

One day, in retrospect, the years of struggle will strike you as the most beautiful.

Ψ

One thing only do I know for certain and that is that man's judgments of value follow directly his wishes for happiness-that, accordingly, they are an attempt to support his illusions with arguments.

Ψ

Our memory has no guarantees at all, and yet we bow more often than is objectively justified to the compulsion to believe what it says.

Ψ

Our possibilities of happiness are already restricted by our constitution. Unhappiness is much less difficult to experience. We are threatened with suffering from three directions: from our own body, which is doomed to decay and dissolution and which cannot even do without pain and anxiety as warning signals; from the external world, which may rage against us with overwhelming and merciless forces of destruction; and finally from our relations to other men. The suffering which comes from this last source is perhaps more painful to us than any other. Out of your vulnerabilities will come your strength.

Ψ

Poets are masters of us ordinary men, in the knowledge of the mind, because they drink at streams which we have not yet made accessible to science.

Ψ

Public self is a conditioned construct of the inner psychological self.

Ψ

Religion is a system of wishful illusions together with a disavowal of reality, such as we find nowhere else but in a state of blissful hallucinatory confusion. Religion's eleventh commandment is "Thou shalt not question".

Ψ

Religion is an attempt to get control over the sensory world, in which we are placed, by means of the wish-world, which we have developed inside us as a result of biological and psychological necessities. But it cannot achieve its end. Its doctrines carry with them the stamp of the times in which they originated, the ignorant childhood days of the human race. Its consolations deserve no trust. Experience teaches us that the world is not a nursery. The ethical commands, to which religion seeks to lend its weight, require some other foundations instead, for human society cannot do without them, and it is dangerous to link up obedience to them with religious belief. If one attempts to assign to religion its place in man's evolution, it seems not so much to be a lasting acquisition, as a parallel to the neurosis which the civilized individual must pass through on his way from childhood to maturity.

Ψ

Religion is an illusion and it derives its strength from the fact that it falls in with our instinctual desires.

Ψ

Religion is comparable to a childhood neurosis, and he is optimistic enough to suppose that mankind will surmount this neurotic phase, just as so many children grow out of their similar neurosis.

Ψ

Religious doctrines are all illusions, they do not admit of proof, and no one can be compelled to consider them as true or to believe in them.

Ψ

Smoking is indispensable if one has nothing to kiss.

Ψ

That feeling of oneness with the universe which is its ideational content sounds very like a first attempt at the consolations of religion, like another way taken by the ego of denying the dangers it sees threatening it in the external world.

*The behavior of a human being in sexual matters
is often a prototype for the whole of his other
modes of reaction in life.*

Ψ

*The challenge of leadership is to be strong, but
not rude; be kind, but not weak; be bold, but not
bully; be thoughtful, but not lazy; be humble, but
not timid; be proud, but not arrogant; have
humor but without folly.*

Ψ

*The child takes his play very seriously and he
expends large amounts of emotion on it.
The creative writer does the same as the child at
play; he creates a world of fantasy which he takes
very seriously.*

Ψ

*The dream is the liberation of the spirit from the
pressure of external nature, a detachment of the
soul from the fetters of matter. The ego is not
master in its own house.*

Ψ

*The ego refuses to be distressed by the
provocations of reality, to let itself be compelled*

*to suffer. It insists that it cannot be affected by the
traumas of the external world; it shows, in fact,
that such traumas are no more than occasions for
it to gain pleasure.*

Ψ

*The goal of all life is death. The great question
that has never been answered, and which I have
not yet been able to answer, despite my thirty
years of research into the feminine soul, is 'What
does a woman want?'*

Ψ

*The individual does actually carry on a double
existence: one designed to serve his own purposes
and another as a link in a chain, in which he
serves against, or at any rate without, any
volition of his own.*

Ψ

*The intention that man should be happy is not in
the plan of Creation.*

Ψ

*The interpretation of dreams is the royal road to a
knowledge of the unconscious activities of the
mind.*

The liberty of the individual is no gift of civilization. It was greatest before there was any civilization.

Ψ

The madman is a dreamer awake.

Ψ

The mind is like an iceberg, it floats with one-seventh of its bulk above water.

Ψ

The more perfect a person is on the outside, the more demons they have on the inside.

Ψ

The only person with whom you have to compare yourself is you in the past.

Ψ

The time comes when each of us has to give up as illusions the expectations which, in his youth, he pinned upon his fellow-men, and when he may learn how much difficulty and pain has been added to his life by their ill-will.

Ψ

The virtuous man contents himself with dreaming that which the wicked man does in actual life. There are no mistakes.

Ψ

There is a powerful force within us, an unilluminated part of the mind – separate from the conscious mind that is constantly at work molding our thought, feelings, and actions.

Ψ

Thought is action in rehearsal.

Ψ

Unexpressed emotions will never die. They are buried alive and will come forth later in uglier ways.

Ψ

We are never so defenseless against suffering as when we love.

Ψ

We are what we are because we have been what we have been, and what is needed for solving the problems of human life and motives is not moral estimates but more knowledge.

Ψ

We choose not randomly each other. We meet only those who already exist in our subconscious.

Ψ

We may insist as often as we like that man's intellect is powerless in comparison to his instinctual life, and we may be right in this. Nevertheless, there is something peculiar about this weakness. The voice of the intellect is a soft one, but it will not rest until it has gained a hearing. Finally, after a countless succession of rebuffs, it succeeds.

Ψ

What is common in all these dreams is obvious. They completely satisfy wishes excited during the day which remain unrealized. They are simply and undisguisedly realizations of wishes.

Ψ

What progress we are making. In the Middle Ages, they would have burned me. Now they are content with burning my books.

Ψ

*When a love-relationship is at its height there is
no room left for any interest in the environment; a
pair of lovers are sufficient to themselves.*

Ψ

*When I am criticized, I can defend myself, but I'm
powerless against the praise.*

Ψ

*When making a decision of minor importance, I
have always found it advantageous to consider all
the pros and cons. In vital matters, however, such
as the choice of a mate or a profession, the
decision should come from the unconscious, from
somewhere within ourselves. In the important
decisions of personal life, we should be governed,
I think, by the deep inner needs of our nature.*

Ψ

*When one does not have what one wants, one
must want what one has.*

Ψ

*Where does a thought go when it's forgotten?
Where Id is, there shall Ego be.*

Ψ

Where such men love they have no desire and where they desire they cannot love.

Ψ

Where the questions of religion are concerned people are guilty of every possible kind of insincerity and intellectual misdemeanor.

Ψ

Whoever loves becomes humble. Those who love have, so to speak, pawned a part of their narcissism.

Ψ

Words and magic were in the beginning one and the same thing and even today words retain much of their magical power.

Ψ

Words have magical power. They can bring either the greatest happiness or deepest despair; they can transfer knowledge from teacher to student; words enable the orator to sway his audience and dictate its decisions. Words are capable of arousing the strongest emotions and prompting all men's actions.

Ψ

You wanted to kill your father in order to be your father yourself. Now you are your father, but a dead father.

Ψ

Carl Gustav Jung Quotes

A creative person has little power over his own life. He is not free. He is captive and driven by his daimon.A dream is a small hidden door in the deepest and most intimate sanctum of the soul, which opens up to that primeval cosmic night that was the soul, long before there was the conscious ego.

Ψ

A dream that is not understood remains a mere occurrence; understood it becomes a living experience.

Ψ

A man who has not passed through the inferno of his passions has never overcome them. As far as we can discern, the sole purpose of human existence is to kindle a light in the darkness of mere being.

Ψ

Everything that irritates us about others can lead us to an understanding of ourselves.

Ψ

A special ability means a heavy expenditure of energy in a particular direction, with a consequent drain from some other side of life.

Ψ

About a third of my cases are suffering from no clinically definable neurosis, but from the senselessness and emptiness of their lives. This can be defined as the general neurosis of our times.

Ψ

An understanding heart is everything in a teacher, and cannot be esteemed highly enough. One looks back with appreciation to the brilliant teachers, but with gratitude to those who touched our human feeling. The curriculum is so much necessary raw material, but warmth is the vital element for the growing plant and for the soul of the child.

Ψ

Art is a kind of innate drive that seizes a human being and makes him its instrument. To perform this difficult office it is sometimes necessary for him to sacrifice happiness and everything that makes life worth living for the ordinary human being.

Ψ

As any change must begin somewhere, it is the single individual who will experience it and carry it through. The change must indeed begin with an individual; it might be any one of us. Nobody can afford to look round and to wait for somebody else to do what he is loath to do himself.

Ψ

As far as we can discern, the sole purpose of human existence is to kindle a light of meaning in the darkness of mere being.

Ψ

Be silent and listen: have you recognized your madness and do you admit it? Have you noticed that all your foundations are completely mired in madness? Do you not want to recognize your madness and welcome it in a friendly manner? You wanted to accept everything. So accept madness too. Let the light of your madness shine, and it will suddenly dawn on you. Madness is not to be despised and not to be feared, but instead you should give it life...If you want to find paths, you should also not spurn madness, since it makes up such a great part of your nature...Be glad that you can recognize it, for you will thus avoid becoming its victim. Madness is a special form of the spirit and clings to all teachings and philosophies, but even more to daily life, since life itself is full of craziness and at bottom utterly illogical. Man strives toward reason only so that he can make rules for himself. Life itself has no rules. That is its mystery and its unknown law. What you call knowledge is an attempt to impose something comprehensible on life.

Ψ

Children are educated by what the grown-up is and not by his talk.

Ψ

Creative powers can just as easily turn out to be destructive. It rests solely with the moral personality.

Ψ

Deep down, below the surface of the average man's conscience, he hears a voice whispering, "There is something not right," no matter how much his rightness is supported by public opinion or moral code.

Ψ

Depression is like a woman in black. If she turns up, don't shoo her away. Invite her in, offer her a seat, treat her like a guest and listen to what she wants to say.

Ψ

Don't hold on to someone who's leaving, otherwise you won't meet the one who's coming.

Ψ

Even a happy life cannot be without a measure of darkness, and the word 'happy' would lose its meaning if it were not balanced by sadness. Every form of addiction is bad, no matter whether the narcotic be alcohol, morphine or idealism.

Ψ

Every form of addiction is bad, no matter whether the narcotic be alcohol, morphine or idealism.

Ψ

Every human life contains a potential, if that potential is not fulfilled, then that life was wasted.

Ψ

Every Mother contains her daughter in herself and every daughter her mother and every mother extends backwards into her mother and forwards into her daughter.

Ψ

Everything about other people that doesn't satisfy us helps us to better understand ourselves.

Ψ

Explore daily the will of God.

Ψ

Faith, hope, love, and insight are the highest achievements of human effort. They are found - given- by experience.

Ψ

For better to come, good must stand aside.

Ψ

Great talents are the most lovely and often the most dangerous fruits on the tree of humanity. They hang upon the most slender twigs that are easily snapped off.

Ψ

How can I be substantial if I do not cast a shadow? I must have a dark side also If I am to be whole.

Ψ

I am astonished, disappointed, pleased with myself. I am distressed, depressed, rapturous. I am all these things at once, and cannot add up the sum. I am incapable of determining ultimate worth or worthlessness; I have no judgment about myself and my life. There is nothing I am quite sure about. I have no definite convictions – not about anything, really. I know only that I was born and exist, and it seems to me that I have been carried along. I exist on the foundation or something I do not know.

Ψ

*I am looking forward enormously to getting back
to the sea again, where the overstimulated psyche
can recover in the presence of that infinite peace
and spaciousness.*

Ψ

*I am no longer alone with myself, and I can only
artificially recall the scary and beautiful feeling
of solitude. This is the shadow side of the fortune
of love.*

Ψ

*I don't aspire to be a good man. I aspire to be a
whole man.*

Ψ

*I have always been impressed by the fact that
there are a surprising number of individuals who
never use their minds if they can avoid it, and an
equal number who do use their minds, but in an
amazingly stupid way.*

Ψ

*I have frequently seen people become neurotic
when they content themselves with inadequate or
wrong answers to the questions of life. They seek*

position, marriage, reputation, outward success of money, and remain unhappy and neurotic even when they have attained what they were seeking. Such people are usually confined within too narrow a spiritual horizon. Their life has not sufficient content, sufficient meaning. If they are enabled to develop into more spacious personalities, the neurosis generally disappears.

Ψ

I regret many follies which sprang from my obstinacy; but without that trait I would not have reached my goal. I shall not commit the fashionable stupidity of regarding everything I cannot explain as a fraud.

Ψ

If a man knows more than others, he becomes lonely.

Ψ

If one does not understand a person, one tends to regard him as a fool.

Ψ

If the path before you is clear, you're probably on someone else's.

Ψ

If we feel our way into the human secrets of the sick person, the madness also reveals its system, and we recognize in the mental illness merely an exceptional reaction to emotional problems which are not strange to us.

Ψ

If you are a gifted person, it doesn't mean that you gained something. It means you have something to give back.

Ψ

In all chaos there is a cosmos, in all disorder a secret order.

Ψ

In each of us there is another whom we do not know.

Ψ

Intuition does not denote something contrary to reason, but something outside of the province of reason.

Ψ

It all depends on how we look at things, and not on how things are in themselves. The least of things with a meaning is worth more in life than the greatest of things without it.

Ψ

It is my mind, with its store of images, that gives the world color and sound; and that supremely real and rational certainty which I can "experience" is, in its most simple form, an exceedingly complicated structure of mental images. Thus there is, in a certain sense, nothing that is directly experienced except the mind itself. Everything is mediated through the mind, translated, filtered, allegorized, twisted, even falsified by it. We are [...] enveloped in a cloud of changing and endlessly shifting images.

Ψ

It is often tragic to see how blatantly a man bungles his own life and the lives of others yet remains totally incapable of seeing how much the whole tragedy originates in himself, and how he continually feeds it and keeps it going. Knowing your own darkness is the best method for dealing with the darkness of other people.

Ψ

Knowledge rests not upon truth alone, but upon error also.

Ψ

Life has always seemed to me like a plant that lives on its rhizome. Its true life is invisible, hidden in the rhizome. The part that appears above ground lasts only a single summer. Then it withers away—an ephemeral apparition. When we think of the unending growth and decay of life and civilizations, we cannot escape the impression of absolute nullity. Yet I have never lost a sense of something that lives and endures underneath the eternal flux. What we see is the blossom, which passes. The rhizome remains.

Ψ

Loneliness does not come from having no people about one, but from being unable to communicate the things that seem important to oneself, or from holding certain views which others find inadmissible.

Ψ

Midlife is the time to let go of an overdominant ego and to contemplate the deeper significance of human existence.

Ψ

Mistakes are, after all, the foundations of truth, and if a man does not know what a thing is, it is at least an increase in knowledge if he knows what it is not.

Ψ

My whole being was seeking for something still unknown which might confer meaning upon the banality of life.

Ψ

Neurosis is always a substitute for legitimate suffering.

Ψ

Nights through dreams tell the myths forgotten by the day.

Ψ

No tree, it is said, can grow to heaven unless its roots reach down to hell.

Ψ

Nobody can fall so low unless he has a great depth. If such a thing can happen to a man, it challenges his best and highest on the other side; that is to say, this depth corresponds to a potential height, and the blackest darkness to a hidden light.

Ψ

Nobody, as long as he moves among the chaotic currents of life, is without trouble. Nothing has a stronger influence psychologically on their environment and especially on their children than the unlived life of the parent.

Ψ

Often the hands will solve a mystery that the intellect has struggled with in vain.

Ψ

One does not become enlightened by imagining figures of light but by making the darkness conscious.

Ψ

People will do anything, no matter how absurd, to avoid facing their own souls.

Ψ

Sensation tells us a thing is. Thinking tells us what it is this thing is. Feeling tells us what this thing is to us.

Ψ

Shame is a soul eating emotion.

Ψ

Show me a sane man and I will cure him for you.

Ψ

Sometimes you have to do something unforgivable just to be able to go on living.

Ψ

Sometimes, indeed, there is such a discrepancy between the genius and his human qualities that one has to ask oneself whether a little less talent might not have been better.

Ψ

Somewhere, right at the bottom of one's own being, one generally does know where one should go and what one should do. But there are times when the clown we call "I" behaves in such a distracting fashion that the inner voice cannot make its presence felt.

Ψ

That which compels us to create a substitute for ourselves is not the external lack of objects, but our incapacity to lovingly include a thing outside of ourselves.

Ψ

The acceptance of oneself is the essence of the whole moral problem and the epitome of a whole outlook on life. That I feed the hungry, that I forgive an insult, that I love my enemy in the name of Christ — all these are undoubtedly great virtues. What I do unto the least of my brethren, that I do unto Christ. But what if I should discover that the least among them all, the poorest of all the beggars, the most impudent of all the offenders, the very enemy himself — that these are within me, and that I myself stand in need of the alms of my own kindness — that I myself am the enemy who must be loved — what then? As a rule, the Christian's attitude is then reversed; there is no longer any question of love or long-suffering; we say to the brother within us "Raca," and condemn and rage against ourselves. We hide it from the world; we refuse to admit ever having met this least among the lowly in ourselves.

Ψ

The best political, social, and spiritual work we can do is to withdraw the projection of our shadow onto others.

Ψ

The bigger the crowd, the more negligible the individual.

Ψ

The capacity for directed thinking I call intellect; the capacity for passive or undirected thinking I call intellectual intuition.

Ψ

The creation of something new is not accomplished by the intellect but by the play instinct acting from inner necessity. The creative mind plays with the objects it loves.

Ψ

The decisive question for man is: Is he related to something infinite or not? That is the telling question of his life. Only if we know that the thing which truly matters is the infinite can we avoid fixing our interests upon futilities, and upon all kinds of goals which are not of real importance.

Ψ

Thus we demand that the world grant us recognition for qualities which we regard as personal possessions: our talent or our beauty. The more a man lays stress on false possessions, and the less sensitivity he has for what is essential, the less satisfying is his life. He feels limited because he has limited aims, and the result is envy and jealousy. If we understand and feel that here in this life we already have a link with the infinite, desires and attitudes change.

Ψ

The fact that a man who goes his own way ends in ruin means nothing...He must obey his own law, as if it were a daemon whispering to him of new and wonderful paths...There are not a few who are called awake by the summons of the voice, whereupon they are at once set apart from the others, feeling themselves confronted with a problem about which the others know nothing. In most cases it is impossible to explain to the others what has happened, for any understanding is walled off by impenetrable prejudices. "You are no different from anybody else," they will chorus or, "there's no such thing," and even if there is such a thing, it is immediately branded as "morbid"...He is at once set apart and isolated, as he has resolved to obey the law that commands him from within. "His own law!" everybody will cry. But he knows better: it is the law...The only meaningful life is a life that strives for the individual realization–absolute and unconditional–of its own particular law...To the extent that a man is untrue to the law of his being...he has failed to realize his own life's meaning.

Ψ

The first half of life is devoted to forming a healthy ego, the second half is going inward and letting go of it.

Ψ

The gods have become our diseases.

Ψ

The greatest and most important problems of life are all fundamentally insoluble. They can never be solved but only outgrown.

Ψ

The greatest tragedy of the family is the unlived lives of the parents.

Ψ

The healthy man does not torture others – generally it is the tortured who turn into torturers.

Ψ

The highest, most decisive experience is to be alone with one's own self. You must be alone to find out what supports you, when you find that you can not support yourself. Only this experience can give you an indestructible foundation.

Ψ

The least of things with a meaning is worth more in life than the greatest of things without it.

Ψ

The majority of my patients consisted not of believers but of those who had lost their faith. The meeting of two personalities is like the contact of two chemical substances: if there is any reaction, both are transformed.

Ψ

The most terrifying thing is to accept oneself completely.

Ψ

The pendulum of the mind oscillates between sense and nonsense, not between right and wrong. The privilege of a lifetime is to become who you truly are.

Ψ

The rational attitude which permits us to declare objective values as valid at all is not the work of the individual subject, but the product of human history.

Ψ

The reason for evil in the world is that people are not able to tell their stories.

Ψ

The shoe that fits one person pinches another; there is no recipe for living that suits all cases.

Ψ

The sight of a child...will arouse certain longings in adult, civilized persons — longings which relate to the unfulfilled desires and needs of those parts of the personality which have been blotted out of the total picture in favor of the adapted persona.

Ψ

The true leader is always led.

Ψ

There are as many nights as days, and the one is just as long as the other in the year's course. Even a happy life cannot be without a measure of darkness, and the word 'happy' would lose its meaning if it were not balanced by sadness.

Ψ

There can be no transforming of darkness into light and of apathy into movement without emotion.

Ψ

There is no coming to consciousness without pain.

Ψ

Thinking is difficult, that's why most people judge.

Ψ

Thoroughly unprepared, we take the step into the afternoon of life. Worse still, we take this step with the false presupposition that our truths and our ideals will serve us as hitherto. But we cannot live the afternoon of life according to the program of life's morning, for what was great in the morning will be little at evening and what in the morning was true, at evening will have become a lie.

Ψ

Through pride we are ever deceiving ourselves. But deep down below the surface of the average conscience a still, small voice says to us, something is out of tune.

Ψ

To ask the right question is already half the solution of a problem.

Ψ

To find out what is truly individual in ourselves, profound reflection is needed; and suddenly we realize how uncommonly difficult the discovery of individuality is.

Ψ

*To me dreams are part of nature, which harbors
no intention to deceive but expresses something
as best it can.*

Ψ

*Until you make the unconscious conscious, it will
direct your life and you will call it fate.*

Ψ

*We cannot change anything until we accept it.
Condemnation does not liberate, it oppresses.*

Ψ

*We may think that we fully control ourselves.
However, a friend can easily reveal something
about us that we have absolutely no idea about.*

Ψ

*We meet ourselves time and again in a thousand
disguises on the path of life.*

Ψ

*We no longer live on what we have, but on
promises, no longer in the present day, but in the
darkness of the future, which, we expect, will at
last bring the proper sunrise. We refuse to
recognize that everything better is purchased at
the price of something worse; that, for example,*

the hope of grater freedom is canceled out by increased enslavement to the state, not to speak of the terrible perils to which the most brilliant discoveries of science expose us. The less we understand of what our [forebears] sought, the less we understand ourselves, and thus we help with all our might to rob the individual of his roots and his guiding instincts, so that he becomes a particle in the mass, ruled only by what Neitzche called the spirit of gravity.

Ψ

We should not pretend to understand the world only by the intellect; we apprehend it just as much by feeling. Therefore, the judgment of the intellect is, at best, only the half of truth, and must, if it be honest, also come to an understanding of its inadequacy.

Ψ

What you resist, persists.

Ψ

Whatever is rejected from the self, appears in the world as an event.

Ψ

*When we consider the infinite variety of dreams,
it is difficult to conceive that there could ever be a
method or a technical procedure which would
lead to an infallible result. It is, indeed, a good
thing that no valid method exists for otherwise
the meaning of the dream would be limited in
advance and would lose precisely that virtue
which makes dreams so valuable for therapeutic
purposes – their ability to offer new points of
view. Where love rules, there is no will to power,
and where power predominates, love is lacking.
The one is the shadow of the other.*

Ψ

*Where wisdom reigns, there is no conflict between
thinking and feeling.*

Ψ

*Whether they apply themselves to good things or
to bad. And if this is lacking, no teacher can
supply it or take its place.*

Ψ

*Who looks outside, dreams; who looks inside,
awakes.*

Ψ

*Wholeness is not achieved by cutting off a portion
of one's being, but by integration of the
contraries.*

Ψ

*With a truly tragic delusion, these theologians fail
to see that it is not a matter of proving the
existence of the light, but of blind people who do
not know that their eyes could see. It is high time
we realized that it is pointless to praise the light
and preach it if nobody can see it. It is much more
needful to teach people the art of seeing.*

Ψ

*Without this playing with fantasy, no creative
work has ever yet come to birth. The debt we owe
to the play of the imagination is incalculable.*

Ψ

*Words are animals, alive with a will of their own.
You are what you do, not what you say you'll do.*

Ψ

*Your perception will become clear only when you
can look into your soul. Your visions will become
clear only when you can look into your own
heart.*

Ψ

Who looks outside, dreams; who looks inside,
awakes.

Ψ

Alfred Adler Quotes

A lie would have no sense unless the truth were felt as dangerous.

Ψ

A simple rule in dealing with those who are hard to get along with is to remember that this person is striving to assert his superiority, and you must deal with him from that point of view.

Death is really a great blessing for humanity, without it there could be no real progress. People who lived for ever would not only hamper and discourage the young, but they would themselves lack sufficient stimulus to be creative.

Ψ

Exaggerated sensitiveness is an expression of the feeling of inferiority.

Ψ

Follow your heart but take your brain with you. Imperfect preparation gives rise to the thousand-fold forms that express physical and mental inferiority and insecurity.

Ψ

It is easier to fight for principles than to live up to them.

Ψ

Meanings are not determined by situations, but we determine ourselves by the meanings we give to situations.

Ψ

Men of genius are admired, men of wealth are envied, men of power are feared; but only men of character are trusted

Ψ

Nobody adopts antisocial behaviour unless they fear that they will fail if they remain on the social side of life.

Ψ

Our modern states are preparing for war without even knowing the future enemy.

Ψ

The chief danger in life is taking too many precautions.

Ψ

The educator must believe in the potential power of his pupil, and he must employ all his art in seeking to bring his pupil to experience this power.

Ψ

The greater the feeling of inferiority that has been experienced, the more powerful is the urge to conquest and the more violent the emotional agitation.

Ψ

The only normal people are the ones you don't know very well.

Ψ

There is a Law that man should love his neighbor as himself. In a few hundred years it should be as natural to mankind as breathing or the upright gait; but if he does not learn it he must perish.

There is no such thing as talent. There is pressure.

Ψ

Trust only movement. Life happens at the level of events, not of words. Trust movement.

Ψ

We are not determined by our experiences, but are self-determined by the meaning we give to them; and when we take particular experiences as the basis for our future life, we are almost certain to be misguided to some degree. Meanings are not determined by situations. We determine ourselves by the meanings we ascribe to situations.

Ψ

We must interpret a bad temper as a sign of inferiority.

Ψ

Karen Horney Quotes

[The neurotic] feels caught in a cellar with many doors, and whichever door he opens leads only into new darkness. And all the time he knows that others are walking outside in sunshine. I do not believe that one can understand any severe neurosis without recognizing the paralyzing hopelessness which it contains. ... It may be difficult then to see that behind all the odd vanities, demands, hostilities, there is a human being who suffers, who feels forever excluded from all that makes life desirable, who knows that even if he gets what he wants he cannot enjoy it.

When one recognizes the existence of all this hopelessness it should not be difficult to understand what appears to be an excessive aggressiveness or even meanness, unexplainable by the particular situation. A person so shut out from every possibility of happiness would have to be a veritable angel if he did not feel hatred toward a world he cannot belong to.

Ψ

A perfectly normal person is rare in our civilization.

Ψ

Concern should drive us into action, not into a depression.

Ψ

I come from a great home and fully supportive family that helped to nurture my dreams. A lot of people don't have those same things in their household.

Ψ

If you want to be proud of yourself, then do things in which you can take pride.

Ψ

*To find a mountain path all by oneself gives a
greater feeling of strength than to take a path that
is shown.*

Ψ

*A perfectly normal person is rare in our
civilization.*

Ψ

*Rationalization may be defined as self-deception
by reasoning.*

Ψ

*Concern should drive us into action, not into a
depression.*

Ψ

*No one ... can entirely step out of his time, that
despite his keenness of vision his thinking is in
many ways bound to be influenced by the
mentality of his time.*

Ψ

*Is not the tremendous strength in men of the
impulse to creative work in every field precisely
due to their feeling of playing a relatively small
part in the creation of living beings, which*

constantly impels them to an overcompensation in achievement?

Ψ

Life itself still remains a very effective therapist.. Like all sciences and all valuations, the psychology of women has hitherto been considered only from the point of view of men The perfect normal person is rare in our civilization.

Ψ

We are too ready to accept others and ourselves as we are and to assume that we are incapable of change. We forget the idea of growth, or we do not take it seriously. There is no good reason why we should not develop and change until the last day we live. Psychoanalysis is one of the most powerful means of helping us to realize this aim.

Ψ

Viktor Frankl Quotes

A man who becomes conscious of the responsibility he bears toward a human being who affectionately waits for him, or to an unfinished work, will never be able to throw away his life. He knows the "why" for his existence, and will be able to bear almost any "how".

Ψ

An abnormal reaction to an abnormal situation is normal behavior.

Ψ

But there was no need to be ashamed of tears, for tears bore witness that a man had the greatest of courage, the courage to suffer.

Ψ

But there was no need to be ashamed of tears, for tears bore witness that a man had the greatest of courage, the courage to suffer.

Ψ

By making him aware of what he can be and of what he should become, he makes these potentialities come true.

Ψ

Don't aim at success. The more you aim at it and make it a target, the more you are going to miss it.

Ψ

For success, like happiness, cannot be pursued; it must ensue, and it only does so as the unintended side effect of one's personal dedication to a cause greater than oneself or as the by-product of one's surrender to a person other than oneself.

Ψ

Everything can be taken from a man but one thing: the last of the human freedoms – to choose one's attitude in any given set of circumstances, to choose one's own way.

Ψ

For the first time in my life, I saw the truth as it is set into song by so many poets, proclaimed as the final wisdom by so many thinkers.

Ψ

For the first time in my life, I saw the truth as it is set into song by so many poets, proclaimed as the final wisdom by so many thinkers. The truth – that Love is the ultimate and highest goal to which man can aspire. Then I grasped the meaning of the greatest secret that human poetry and human thought and belief have to impart: The salvation of man is through love and in love.

Ψ

Forces beyond your control can take away everything you possess except one thing, your freedom to choose how you will respond to the situation.

Ψ

Happiness cannot be pursued; it must ensue. Happiness must happen, and the same holds for success: you have to let it happen by not caring about it. I want you to listen to what your conscience commands you to do and go on to carry it out to the best of your knowledge.

Ψ

I do not forget any good deed done to me and I do not carry a grudge for a bad one.

Ψ

I recommend that the Statue of Liberty on the East Coast be supplemented by a Statue of Responsibility on the West Coast.

Ψ

If there is meaning in life at all, then there must be meaning in suffering.

Ψ

If we take man as he really is, we make him worse. But if we overestimate him…we promote him to what he really can be.

Ψ

In some ways suffering ceases to be suffering at the moment it finds a meaning, such as the meaning of a sacrifice.

Ψ

In some ways suffering ceases to be suffering at the moment it finds a meaning, such as the meaning of a sacrifice.

Ψ

It did not really matter what we expected from life, but rather what life expected from us. We needed to stop asking about the meaning of life, and instead to think of ourselves as those who were being questioned by life – daily and hourly. Our answer must consist, not in talk and meditation, but in right action and in right conduct.

Ψ

It did not really matter what we expected from life, but rather what life expected from us. We needed to stop asking about the meaning of life, and instead to think of ourselves as those who were being questioned by life—daily and hourly. It is not freedom from conditions, but it is freedom to take a stand toward the conditions.

Ψ

Life is never made unbearable by circumstances, but only by lack of meaning and purpose.

Ψ

Love goes very far beyond the physical person of the beloved. It finds its deepest meaning in his spiritual being, his inner self. Whether or not he is actually present, whether or not he is still alive at all, ceases somehow to be of importance.

Ψ

Love is the only way to grasp another human being in the innermost core of his personality. No one can become fully aware of the very essence of another human being unless he loves him. By his love he is able to see the essential traits and features in the beloved person; and even more, he sees that which is potential in him, which is not yet actualized but yet ought to be actualized.

Ψ

Man does not simply exist but always decides what his existence will be, what he will become the next moment. By the same token, every human being has the freedom to change at any instant.

Ψ

No man should judge unless he asks himself in absolute honest whether in a similar situation he might not have done the same.

Ψ

Our answer must consist, not in talk and meditation, but in right action and in right conduct. Life ultimately means taking the responsibility to find the right answer to its problems and to fulfill the tasks which it constantly sets for each individual.

Ψ

Our greatest freedom is the freedom to choose our attitude.

Ψ

So live as if you were living already for the second time and as if you had acted the first time as wrongly as you are about to act now!

Ψ

The attempt to develop a sense of humor and to see things in a humorous light is some kind of a trick learned while mastering the art of living. Yet it is possible to practice the art of living even in a concentration camp, although suffering is omnipresent.

Ψ

The consciousness of one's inner value is anchored in higher, more spiritual things, and cannot be shaken by camp life. But how many free men, let alone prisoners possess it?

Ψ

The one thing you can't take away from me is the way I choose to respond to what you do to me. The last of one's freedoms is to choose one's attitude in any given circumstance.

Ψ

The one thing you can't take away from me is the way I choose to respond to what you do to me. The last of one's freedoms is to choose one's attitude in any given circumstance.

Ψ

The pessimist resembles a man who observes with fear and sadness that his wall calendar, from which he daily tears a sheet, grows thinner with each passing day.

Ψ

Those who have a 'why' to live, can bear with almost any 'how'.

Ψ

To draw an analogy: a man's suffering is similar to the behavior of a gas. If a certain quantity of

*gas is pumped into an empty chamber, it will fill
the chamber completely and evenly, no matter
how big the chamber. Thus suffering completely
fills the human soul and conscious mind, no
matter whether the suffering is great or little.
Therefore the "size" of human suffering is
absolutely relative.*

Ψ

*Today's society is characterized by achievement
orientation, and consequently it adores people
who are successful and happy and, in particular,
it adores the young. It virtually ignores the value
of all those who are otherwise, and in doing so
blurs the decisive difference being valuable in the
sense of dignity and being valuable in the sense of
usefulness. If one is not cognizant of this
difference and holds that an individual's value
stems only from his present usefulness, then,
believe me, one owes it only to personal
inconsistency not to plead for euthanasia along
the lines of Hitler's program, that is to say,
'mercy' killing of all those who have lost their
social usefulness, be it because of old age,
incurable illness, mental deterioration, or
whatever handicap they may suffer.*

Ψ

Ultimately, the man should not ask what the meaning of his life is, but rather must recognize that it is he who is asked. In a word, each man is questioned by life; and he can only answer to life by answering for his own life; to life, he can only respond by being responsible.

Ψ

We who lived in concentration camps can remember the men who walked through the huts comforting others, giving away their last piece of bread.

Ψ

What is to give light must endure burning.

Ψ

When we are no longer able to change a situation, we are challenged to change ourselves.

Ψ

Erik Berne Quotes

*A healthy person goes 'Yes,' 'No,' and 'Whoopee!'
An unhealthy person goes 'Yes, but,' 'No, but,'
and 'No whoopee.' A loser doesn't know what
he'll do if he loses but talks about what he'll do if
he wins and a winner doesn't talk about what
he'll do if he wins but knows what he'll do if he
loses.*

Ψ

*Awareness requires living in the here and now,
and not in the elsewhere, the past or the future.*

Ψ

Each person designs his own life, freedom gives him the power to carry out his own designs, and power gives the freedom to interfere with the designs of others.

Ψ

Games are a compromise between intimacy and keeping intimacy away.

Ψ

I'm OK, and so are you.

Ψ

No man is a hero to his wife's psychiatrist.

Ψ

The destiny of every human being is decided by what goes on inside his skull when confronted by what goes on outside his skull.

Ψ

The moment a little boy is concerned with which is a jay and which is a sparrow, he can no longer see the birds or hear them sing.

Ψ

We are born princes and the civilizing process makes us frogs.

Carl Rodgers Quotes

A second characteristic of the process which for me is the good life, is that it involves an increasingly tendency to live fully in each moment. I believe it would be evident that for the person who was fully open to his new experience, completely without defensiveness, each moment would be new.
Change threatens, and its possibility creates frightened, angry people. They are found in their purest essence on the extreme right, but in all of us there is some fear of process, of change.

Ψ

Evaluation by others is not a guide for me. The judgments of others, while they are to be listened to, and taken into account for what they are, can never be a guide for me. This has been a hard thing to learn.

Ψ

Experience is, for me, the highest authority. The touchstone of validity is my own experience. No other person's ideas, and none of my own ideas, are as authoritative as my experience. It is to experience that I must return again and again, to discover a closer approximation to truth as it is in the process of becoming in me. Neither the Bible nor the prophets — neither Freud nor research — neither the revelations of God nor man — can take precedence over my own direct experience. My experience is not authoritative because it is infallible. It is the basis of authority because it can always be checked in new primary ways. In this way its frequent error or fallibility is always open to correction.

Ψ

I am isolated. I sit in a glass ball, I see people through a glass wall. I scream, but they do not hear me.

Ψ

I am less and less a creature of influences in myself which operate beyond my ken in the realms of the unconscious. I am increasingly an architect of self. I am free to will and choose. I can, through accepting my individuality, my 'isness,' become more of my uniqueness, more of my potentiality.

Ψ

I believe that individuals nowadays are probably more aware of their inner loneliness than has ever been true before in history.

Ψ

I find it very satisfying when I can be real, when I can be close to whatever it is that is going on within me. I like it when I can listen to myself. To really know what I am experiencing in the moment is by no means an easy thing, but I feel somewhat encouraged because I think that over the years I have been improving at it.

Ψ

I found myself doing this same thing—playing a role of having greater certainty and greater competence than I really possess. I can't tell you how disgusted with myself I felt as I realized what I was doing: I was not being me, I was playing a part.

Ψ

I have come to feel that the only learning which significantly influences behavior is self-discovered, self-appropriated learning.

Ψ

I like to think of myself as a quiet revolutionary.

Ψ

I'm not perfect... But I'm enough.

Ψ

If you are willing to enter his private world and see the way life appears to him, without any attempt to make evaluative judgments, you run the risk of being changed yourself.

Ψ

In my deepest contacts with individuals in therapy, even those whose troubles are most disturbing, whose behavior has been most anti-social, whose feelings seem most abnormal, I find this to be true. When I can sensitively understand the feelings which they are expressing, when I am able to accept them as separate persons in their own right, then I find that they tend to move in certain directions. And what are these directions in which they tend to move? The words which I believe are most truly descriptive are words such as positive, constructive, moving toward self-actualization, growing toward maturity, growing toward socialization.

Ψ

In my early professionals years I was asking the question: How can I treat, or cure, or change this person? Now I would phrase the question in this way: How can I provide a relationship which this person may use for his own personal growth? I have gradually come to one negative conclusion about the good life. It seems to me that the good life is not any fixed state. It is not, in my estimation, a state of virtue, or contentment, or nirvana, or happiness. It is not a condition in which the individual is adjusted or fulfilled or actualized. To use psychological terms, it is not a state of drive-reduction, or tension-reduction, or homeostasis. The good life is a process, not a state of being. It is a direction not a destination.

Ψ

It is so obvious when a person is not hiding behind a facade but is speaking from deep within himself.

Ψ

It is the client who knows what hurts, what directions to go, what problems are crucial, what experiences have been deeply buried. It began to occur to me that unless I had a need to demonstrate my own cleverness and learning, I would do better to rely upon the client for the direction of movement in the process.

Ψ

It seems to me that anything that can be taught to another is relatively inconsequential, and has little or no significant influence on behavior.

Ψ

Once an experience is fully in awareness, fully accepted, then it can be coped with effectively, like any other clear reality.

Ψ

Perhaps partly because of the troubling business of being struggled over, I have come to value highly the privilege of getting away, of being alone. It has seemed to me that my most fruitful periods of work are the times when I have been able to get completely away from what others think, from professional expectations and daily demands, and gain perspective on what I am doing.

Ψ

So while I still hate to readjust my thinking, still hate to give up old ways of perceiving and conceptualizing, yet at some deeper level I have, to a considerable degree, come to realize that these painful reorganizations are what is known as learning.

Ψ

So, here we are, all of us poor bewildered darlings, wandering adrift in a universe too big and too complex for us, clasping and ricochetting off other people too different and too perplexing for us, and seeking to satisfy myriad, shifting, vague needs and desires, both mean and exalted. And sometimes we mesh. Don't we?

Ψ

The conviction grows in me that we shall discover laws of personality and behavior which are as significant for human progress or human understanding as the law of gravity or the laws of thermodynamics.

Ψ

The curious paradox is that when I accept myself just as I am, then I can change.

Ψ

The good life is a process, not a state of being. It is a direction, not a destination." Today we have abundant opportunities to utilize our strengths and passions, do things we enjoy, and connect with people we love.Tomorrow might bring a world of exciting new possibilities, but today, wherever we stand on our journey, can be an adventure in itself.

Ψ

The mainspring of creativity appears to be the same tendency which we discover so deeply as the curative force in psychotherapy—man's tendency to actualize himself, to become his potentialities.

Ψ

The only person who is educated is the one who has learned how to learn and change.

Ψ

The right wing has a large proportion of authoritarian personalities. They tend to believe man is, by nature, basically evil. Surrounded as all of us are by the bigness of impersonal forces which seem beyond our power to control, they look for the 'enemy', so that they can hate him. At different times in history 'the enemy' has been the witch, the demon, the Communist (remember Joe McCarthy?), and now sex education, sensitivity training, 'non-religious humanism', and other current demons.

Ψ

The third facilitative aspect of the relationship is empathic understanding. This means that the therapist senses accurately the feelings and personal meanings that the client is experiencing and communicates this understanding to the client. When functioning best, the therapist is so much inside the private world of the other that he or she can clarify not only the meanings of which the client is aware but even those just below the level of awareness. This kind of sensitive, active listening is exceedingly rare in our lives. We think we listen, but very rarely do we listen with real understanding, true empathy. Yet listening, of this very special kind, is one of the most potent forces for change that I know.

Ψ

The very essence of the creative is its novelty, and hence we have no standard by which to judge it.

Ψ

There is direction but there is no destination.

Ψ

We cannot change, we cannot move away from what we are until we thoroughly accept what we are. Then change seems to come about almost unnoticed.

Ψ

*We live by a perceptual "map" which is never
reality itself.*

Ψ

*What I am is good enough if I would only be it
openly.*

Ψ

What is most personal is most universal.

Ψ

*When I am thus able to be in process, it is clear
that there can be no closed system of beliefs, no
unchanging set of principles which I hold. Life is
guided by a changing understanding of and
interpretation of my experience. It is always in
process of becoming.*

Ψ

*When I have been listened to and when I have
been heard, I am able to re-perceive my world in
a new way and to go on. It is astonishing how
elements that seem insoluble become soluble
when someone listens, how confusions that seem
irremediable turn into relatively clear flowing
streams when one is heard. I have deeply*

appreciated the times that I have experienced this sensitive, empathic, concentrated listening.

Ψ

When I look at a sunset as I did the other evening, I don't find myself saying, "Soften the orange a little on the right hand corner, and put a bit more purple along the base, and use a little more pink in the cloud color." I don't do that. I don't try to control a sunset. I watch it with awe as it unfolds. I like myself best when I can appreciate my staff member, my son, my daughter, my grandchildren, in this same way. I believe this is a somewhat Oriental attitude; for me it is a most satisfying one.

Ψ

When I look at the world I'm pessimistic, but when I look at people I am optimistic.

Ψ

When you are in psychological distress and someone really hears you without passing judgement on you, without trying to take responsibility for you, without trying to mold you, it feels damn good!

Ψ

*You can't possibly be afraid of death, really, you
can only be afraid of life.*

Ψ

Abraham Maslow Quotes

A musician must make music, an artist must paint, a poet must write if he is to be ultimately at peace with himself. What a man can be, he must be.

Ψ

All of life is education and everybody is a teacher and everybody is forever a pupil.

Ψ

Appreciate again and again, freshly and naively the basic goods of life, with awe, pleasure, wonder and even ecstasy, however stable these experiences may have become to others.

Ψ

Be independent of the good opinion of other people.

Ψ

But behavior in the human being is sometimes a defense, a way of concealing motives and thoughts, as language can be a way of hiding your thoughts and preventing communication.

Ψ

Creativity is a characteristic given to all human beings at birth.

Ψ

Don't worry when you are not recognized but strive to be worthy of recognition.

Ψ

Every human being has both sets of forces within him. One set clings to safety and defensiveness out of fear, tending to regress backward, hanging on to the past, afraid to grow away from the primitive communication with the mother's uterus and breast, afraid to take chances, afraid to jeopardize what he already has, afraid of independence, freedom, and separateness. The other set of forces impels him forward toward wholeness of Self and uniqueness of Self, toward full functioning of all his capacities, toward confidence in the face of the external world at the same time that he can accept his deepest, real, unconscious Self.

Ψ

False optimism sooner or later means disillusionment, anger and hopelessness.

Ψ

Growth must be chosen again and again; fear must be overcome again and again.

Ψ

I can feel guilty about the past, apprehensive about the future, but only in the present can I act. The ability to be in the present moment is a major component of mental wellness.

Ψ

I have learned the novice can often see things that the expert overlooks. All that is necessary is not to be afraid of making mistakes, or of appearing naive.

Ψ

*I suppose it is tempting, if the only tool you have
is a hammer, to treat everything as if it were a
nail.*

Ψ

*I'm someone who likes plowing new ground, then
walking away from it. I get bored easily. For me,
the big thrill comes with discovering.*

Ψ

*If I were dropped out of a plane into the ocean
and told the nearest land was a thousand miles
away, I'd still swim. And I'd despise the one who
gave up.*

Ψ

*If the essential core of the person is denied or
suppressed, he gets sick sometimes in obvious
ways, sometimes in subtle ways, sometimes
immediately, sometimes later.*

Ψ

*If the only tool you have is a hammer, you tend to
see every problem as a nail.*

Ψ

*If you plan on being anything less than what you
are capable of being, you will probably be
unhappy all the days of your life.*

Ψ

*In any given moment we have two options: to step
forward into growth or to step back into safety.*

Ψ

*It is as necessary for man to live in beauty rather
than ugliness as it is necessary for him to have
food for an aching belly or rest for a weary body.*

Ψ

*It isn't normal to know what we want. It is a rare
and difficult psychological achievement.*

Ψ

*It looks as if there were a single ultimate goal for
mankind, a far goal toward which all persons
strive. This is called variously by different
authors self-actualization, self-realization,
integration, psychological health, individuation,
autonomy, creativity, productivity, but they all
agree that this amounts to realizing the
potentialities of the person, that is to say,*

becoming fully human, everything that person can be.

Ψ

It seems that the necessary thing to do is not to fear mistakes, to plunge in, to do the best that one can, hoping to learn enough from blunders to correct them eventually.

Ψ

Let people realize clearly that every time they threaten someone or humiliate or unnecessarily hurt or dominate or reject another human being, they become forces for the creation of psychopathology, even if these be small forces. Let them recognize that every person who is kind, helpful, decent, psychologically democratic, affectionate, and warm, is a psychotherapeutic force, even though a small one.

Ψ

Life is an ongoing process of choosing between safety (out of fear and need for defense) and risk (for the sake of progress and growth). Make the growth choice a dozen times a day.

Ψ

Not allowing people to go through their pain, and protecting them from it, may turn out to be a kind of over-protection, which in turn implies a certain lack of respect for the integrity and the intrinsic nature and the future development of the individual.

Ψ

One can choose to go back toward safety or forward toward growth. Growth must be chosen again and again; fear must be overcome again and again.

Ψ

One of the goals of education should be to teach that life is precious.

Ψ

One's only rival is one's own potentialities. One's an only failure is failing to live up to one's own possibilities. In this sense, every man can be a king, and must, therefore, be treated like a king.

Ψ

Quitting smoking can be a very good test of one's character. Pass the test and you will have accomplished so much more than just get rid of one bad habit.

Ψ

Religion becomes a state of mind achievable in almost any activity of life if this activity is raised to a suitable level of perfection.

Ψ

Seeing is better than being blind, even when seeing hurts.

Ψ

Self-actualized people…live more in the real world of nature than in the man-made mass of concepts, abstractions, expectations, beliefs, and stereotypes that most people confuse with the world.

Ψ

The ability to be in the present moment is a major component of mental wellness.

Ψ

The best way to view a present problem is to give it all you've got, to study it and its nature, to perceive within it the intrinsic interrelationships, to discover the answer to the problem within the problem itself.

Ψ

The definition of the good society is one in which virtue pays.

Ψ

The fact is that people are good if only their fundamental wishes are satisfied, their wish for affection and security. Give people affection and security, and they will be secure in their feelings and their behavior.

Ψ

The great lesson from the true mystics is that the sacred is in the ordinary, that it is to be found in one's daily life, in one's neighbors, friends, and family, and in one's backyard.

Ψ

The human being needs a framework of values, a philosophy of life, a religion or religion-surrogate to live by and understand by, in about the same sense that he needs sunlight, calcium or love.

Ψ

The key question isn't "What fosters creativity?"
But why in God's name isn't everyone creative?
Where was the human potential lost? How was it
crippled? I think therefore a good question might
not be why do people create? But why do people
not create or innovate?

Ψ

We have got to abandon that sense of amazement
in the face of creativity as if it were a miracle that
anybody created anything. The key question isn't,
what fosters creativity? But it is, why isn't
everyone creative?

Ψ

The most beautiful fate, the most wonderful good
fortune that can happen to any human being, is to
be paid for doing that which
he passionately loves to do.

Ψ

The most fortunate are those who have a
wonderful capacity to appreciate again and
again, freshly and naively, the basic goods of life,
with awe, pleasure, wonder, and even ecstasy.

Ψ

The most stable, and therefore, the most healthy self-esteem is based on deserved respect from others rather than on external fame or celebrity and unwarranted adulation.

Ψ

The only happy people I know are the ones who are working well at something they consider important.

Ψ

The sacred is in the ordinary...it is to be found in one's daily life, in one's neighbors, friends, and family, in one's own backyard...travel may be a flight from confronting the scared–this lesson can be easily lost. To be looking elsewhere for miracles is to be a sure sign of ignorance that everything is miraculous.

Ψ

The science of psychology has been far more successful on the negative than on the positive side. It has revealed to us much about man's shortcomings, his illnesses, his sins, but little about his potentialities, his virtues, his achievable aspirations, or his psychological health.

Ψ

The spiritual life is part of the human essence. It is a defining characteristic of human nature, without which human nature is not fully human.

Ψ

The story of the human race is the story of men and women selling themselves short.

Ψ

To the man who only has a hammer, everything he encounters begins to look like a nail.

Ψ

We fear our highest possibilities. We are generally afraid to become that which we can glimpse in our most perfect moments, under conditions of great courage. We enjoy and even thrill to godlike possibilities we see in ourselves in such peak moments. And yet we simultaneously shiver with weakness, awe, and fear before these very same possibilities.

Ψ

We fear our highest possibility. We are generally afraid to become that which we can glimpse in our most perfect moments.

We need not take refuge in supernatural gods to explain our saints and sages and heroes and statesmen as if to explain our disbelief that mere unaided human beings could be that good or wise.

What a man can be, he must be. This need we call self-actualization.

What is necessary to change a person is to change his awareness of himself.

What one can be, one must be!

When people appear to be something other than good and decent, it is only because they are reacting to stress, pain, or the deprivation of basic human needs such as security, love, and self-esteem.

Erich Fromm Quotes

A person who has not been completely alienated, who has remained sensitive and able to feel, who has not lost the sense of dignity, who is not yet "for sale", who can still suffer over the suffering of others, who has not acquired fully the having mode of existence – briefly, a person who has remained a person and not become a thing – cannot help feeling lonely, powerless, isolated in present-day society. He cannot help doubting himself and his own convictions, if not his sanity. He cannot help suffering, even though he can experience moments of joy and clarity that are absent in the life of his "normal" contemporaries. Not rarely will he suffer from

neurosis that results from the situation of a sane man living in an insane society, rather than that of the more conventional neurosis of a sick man trying to adapt himself to a sick society. In the process of going further in his analysis, i.e. of growing to greater independence and productivity,his neurotic symptoms will cure themselves.

Ψ

All men are in need of help and depend on one another. Human solidarity is the necessary condition for the unfolding of any one individual.

Ψ

As long as anyone believes that his ideal and purpose is outside him, that it is above the clouds, in the past or in the future, he will go outside himself and seek fulfillment where it cannot be found. He will look for solutions and answers at every point except where they can be found – in himself.

Ψ

As we ascend the social ladder, viciousness wears a thicker mask.

Ψ

Attractive' usually means a nice package of qualities which are popular and sought after on the personality market.

Ψ

Both dreams and myths are important communications from ourselves to ourselves. If we do not understand the language in which they are written, we miss a great deal of what we know and tell ourselves in those hours when we are not busy manipulating the outside world.

Ψ

Care and responsibility are constituent elements of love, but without respect for and knowledge of the beloved person, love deteriorates into domination and possessiveness.

Ψ

Creativity requires the courage to let go of certainties.

Ψ

Destructiveness is the outcome of unlived lives.

Ψ

Education makes machines which act like men and produces men who act like machines.

Ψ

Even good deeds by the enemy are considered a sign of particular devilishness, meant to deceive us and the world, while our bad deeds are necessary and justified by our noble goals which they serve.

Ψ

Giving is the highest expression of potency. In the very act of giving, I experience my strength, my wealth, my power. This experience of heightened vitality and potency fills me with joy. I experience myself as overflowing, spending, alive, hence as joyous. Giving is more joyous than receiving, not because it is a deprivation, but because in the act of giving lies the expression of my aliveness.

Ψ

I believe that love is the main key to open the doors to the "growth" of man. Love and union with someone or something outside of oneself, the union that allows one to put oneself into a relationship with others, to feel one with others, without limiting the sense of integrity and independence.

Ψ

I believe that man is the product of natural evolution that is born from the conflict of being a prisoner and separated from nature, and from the need to find unity and harmony with it.

Ψ

I believe that none can 'save' his fellow man by making a choice for him. To help him, he can indicate the possible alternatives, with sincerity and love, without being sentimental and without illusion. The knowledge and awareness of the freeing alternatives can reawaken in an individual all his hidden energies and put him on the path to choosing respect for 'life' instead of for 'death.'

Ψ

I want the loved person to grow and unfold for his own sake, and in his own ways, and not for the purpose of serving me.

Ψ

If a person loves only one other person and is indifferent to all others, his love is not love but a symbiotic attachment, or an enlarged egotism. "If I am what I have and if I lose what I have who then am I?"

Ψ

If other people do not understand our behavior— so what? Their request that we must only do what they understand is an attempt to dictate to us. If this is being "asocial" or "irrational" in their eyes, so be it. Mostly they resent our freedom and our courage to be ourselves. We owe nobody an explanation or an accounting, as long as our acts do not hurt or infringe on them. How many lives have been ruined by this need to "explain," which usually implies that the explanation is "understood," i.e. approved. Let your deeds be judged, and from your deeds, your real intentions, but know that a free person owes an explanation only to himself—to his reason and his conscience —and to the few who may have a justified claim for explanation.

Ψ

Immature love says: 'I love you because I need you.' Mature love says 'I need you because I love you.'

Ψ

In erotic love, two people who were separate become one. In motherly love, two people who were one become separate. The mother must not only tolerate, she must wish and support the child's separation.

Ψ

In love the paradox occurs that two beings become one and yet remain two.

Ψ

In the nineteenth century the problem was that God is dead; in the twentieth century the problem is that man is dead.

Ψ

Infantile love follows the principle: "I love because I am loved.

Ψ

Mature love follows the principle: "I am loved because I love."

Ψ

Immature love says: "I love you because I need you."

Ψ

Mature love says: "I need you because I love you."

Ψ

Is love an art? Then it requires knowledge and effort.

Ψ

It is naively assumed that the fact that the majority of people share certain ideas and feelings proves the validity of these ideas and feelings. Nothing could be further from the truth. Consensual validation as such has no bearing on reason or mental health.

Ψ

Just as love for one individual which excludes the love for others is not love, love for one's country which is not part of one's love for humanity is not love, but idolatrous worship.

Ψ

Just as love is an orientation which refers to all objects and is incompatible with the restriction to one object, so is reason a human faculty which must embrace the whole of the world with which man is confronted.

Ψ

Love is a decision, it is a judgment, it is a promise. If love were only a feeling, there would be no basis for the promise to love each other forever. A feeling comes and it may go. How can I judge that it will stay forever, when my act does not involve judgment and decision.

Ψ

Love is an action, the practice of human power, which can be practiced only in freedom and never as a result of compulsion.

Ψ

Love is not primarily a relationship to a specific person; it is an attitude, an ordination of character which determines the relatedness of the person to the whole world as a whole, not toward one object of love

Ψ

Love is often nothing but a favorable exchange between two people who get the most of what they can expect, considering their value on the personality market.

Ψ

Love is the only sane and satisfactory answer to the problem of human existence.

Ψ

Love isn't something natural. Rather it requires discipline, concentration, patience, faith, and the overcoming of narcissism. It isn't a feeling, it is a practice.

Ψ

Love means to commit oneself without guarantee, to give oneself completely in the hope that our love will produce love in the loved person. Love is an act of faith, and whoever is of little faith is also of little love.

Ψ

Man is born as a freak of nature, being within nature and yet transcending it.

Ψ

Man is the only animal for whom his own existence is a problem which he has to solve and from which he cannot escape.

Ψ

Man is the only animal for whom his own existence is a problem which he has to solve.

Ψ

Man may be defined as the animal that can say "I," that can be aware of himself as a separate entity.

Ψ

Man's main task in life is to give birth to himself, to become what he potentially is. The most important product of his effort is his own personality.

Ψ

"Man's main task is to give birth to himself." "Men are born equal but they are also born different."

Ψ

Modern man has transformed himself into a commodity; he experiences his life energy as an investment with which he should make the highest

*profit, considering his position and the situation
on the personality market. He is alienated from
himself, from his fellow men and from nature. His
main aim is profitable exchange of his skills,
knowledge, and of himself, his "personality
package" with others who are equally intent on a
fair and profitable exchange. Life has no goal
except the one to move, no principle except the
one of fair exchange, no satisfaction except the
one to consume.*

Ψ

*Modern man thinks he loses something – time –
when he does not do things quickly. Yet he does
not know what to do with the time he gains,
except kill it.*

Ψ

*Modern man, if he dared to be articulate about
his concept of heaven, would describe a vision
which would look like the biggest department
store in the world, showing new things and
gadgets, and himself having plenty of money with
which to buy them. He would wander around
open-mouthed in this heaven of gadgets and
commodities, provided only that there were ever*

more and newer things to buy, and perhaps that his neighbors were just a little less privileged than he.

Ψ

Most people die before they are fully born. Creativeness means to be born before one dies.

Ψ

Nationalism is our form of incest, is our idolatry, is our insanity. 'Patriotism' is its cult...Just as love for one individual which excludes the love for others is not love, love for one's country which is not part of one's love for humanity is not love, but idolatrous worship.

Ψ

Neurosis can be understood best as the battle between tendencies within an individual; deep character analysis leads, if successful, to the progressive solution.

Ψ

Not he who has much is rich, but he who gives much.

Ψ

*One cannot be deeply responsive to the world
without being saddened very often.*

Ψ

*Only the person who has faith in himself is able
to be faithful to others.*

Ψ

*Paradoxically, the ability to be alone is the
condition for the ability to love.*

Ψ

*Reason flows from the blending of rational
thought and feeling. If the two functions are torn
apart, thinking deteriorates into schizoid
intellectual activity and feeling deteriorates into
neurotic life-damaging passions.*

Ψ

*Reason is man's faculty for grasping the world by
thought, in contradiction to intelligence, which is
man's ability to manipulate the world with the
help of thought. Reason is man's instrument for
arriving at the truth, intelligence is man's
instrument for manipulating the world more
successfully; the former is essentially human, the
latter belongs to the animal part of man.*

Ψ

Respect is not fear and awe; it denotes, in accordance with the root of the word (respicere = to look at), the ability to see a person as he is, to be aware of his individuality and uniqueness.

Ψ

Robots do not rebel.

Ψ

Selfish persons are incapable of loving others, but they are not capable of loving themselves either.

Ψ

Society must be organized in such a way that man's social, loving nature is not separated from his social existence, but becomes one with it. If it is true, as I have tried to show, that love is the only sane and satisfactory answer to the problem of human existence, then any society which excludes, relatively, the development of love, must in the long run perish of its own contradiction with the basic necessities of human nature.

Ψ

*That millions of people share the same forms of
mental pathology does not make these people
sane.*

Ψ

*The danger of the past was that men became
slaves. The danger of the future is that men may
become robots.*

Ψ

*The existential split in man would be unbearable
could he not establish a sense of unity within
himself and with the natural and human world
outside.*

Ψ

*The fact that millions of people share the same
vices does not make these vices virtues, the fact
that they share so many errors does not make the
errors to be truths, and the fact that millions of
people share the same form of mental pathology
does not make these people sane.*

Ψ

*The faculty to think objectively is reason; the
emotional attitude behind reason is that
of humility. To be objective, to use one's reason,*

is possible only if one has achieved an attitude of humility, if one has emerged from the dreams of omniscience and omnipotence which one has as a child. Love, being dependent on the relative absence of narcissism, requires the developement of humility, objectivity and reason.

Ψ

I must try to see the difference between my picture of a person and his behavior, as it is narcissistically distorted, and the person's reality as it exists regardless of my interests, needs and fears.

Ψ

The main condition for the achievement of love is the overcoming of one's narcissism. The narcissistic orientation is one in which one experiences as real only that which exists within oneself, while the phenomena in the outside world have no reality in themselves, but are experienced only from the viewpoint of their being useful or dangerous to one. The opposite pole to narcissism is objectivity; it is the faculty to see other people and things as they are, objectively, and to be able to separate this objective picture from a picture which is formed by one's desires and fears.

Ψ

The mature response to the problem of existence is love.

Ψ

The narcissistic, the domineering, the possessive woman can succeed in being a "loving" mother as long as the child is small. Only the really loving woman, the woman who is happier in giving than in taking, who is firmly rooted in her own existence, can be a loving mother when the child is in the process of separation.

Ψ

The only truly affluent are those who do not want more than they have.

Ψ

The quest for certainty blocks the search for meaning. Uncertainty is the very condition to impel man to unfold his powers.

Ψ

The real opposition is that between the ego-bound man, whose existence is structured by the principle of having, and the free man, who has overcome his egocentricity.

Ψ

The revolutionary and critical thinker is in a certain way always outside of his society while of course he is at the same time also in it.

Ψ

The sadistic person is as dependent on the submissive person as the latter is on the former; neither can live without the other.

Ψ

The same polarity of the male and female principle exists in nature; not only, as is obvious in animals and plants, but in the polarity of the two fundamental functions, that of receiving and penetrating. It is the polarity of earth and rain, of the river and the ocean, of night and day, of darkness and light, of matter and spirit.

Ψ

The sick individual finds himself at home with all other similarly sick individuals. The whole culture is geared to this kind of pathology. The result is that the average individual does not experience the separateness and isolation the fully schizophrenic person feels. He feels at ease among those who suffer from the same deformation; in fact, it is the fully sane person who feels isolated in the insane society — and he may suffer so much from the incapacity to communicate that it is he who may become psychotic. In the context of this study the crucial question is whether the hypothesis of a quasi-autistic or of low-grade schizophrenic disturbance would help us to explain some of the violence spreading today.

Ψ

The successful revolutionary is a statesman, the unsuccessful one a criminal.

Ψ

There is no meaning to life except the meaning man gives his life by the unfolding of his powers.

Ψ

There is only one meaning of life: the act of living itself.

Ψ

There is perhaps no phenomenon which contains so much destructive feeling as 'moral indignation,' which permits envy or hate to be acted out under the guise of virtue.

Ψ

To die is poignantly bitter, but the idea of having to die without having lived is unbearable.

Ψ

To hope means to be ready at every moment for that which is not yet born, and yet not become desperate if there is no birth in our lifetime.

Ψ

To love one person productively means to be related to his human core, to him as representing mankind. Love for one individual, in so far as it is divorced from love for man, can refer only to the superficial and to the accidental; of necessity it remains shallow.

Ψ

We consume, as we produce, without any concrete relatedness to the objects with which we deal; We live in a world of things, and our only connection with them is that we know how to manipulate or to consume them.

Ψ

What does one person give to another? He gives of himself, of the most precious he has, he gives of his life. This does not necessarily mean that he sacrifices his life for the other – but that he gives him of that which is alive in him; he gives him of his joy, of his interest, of his understanding, of his knowledge, of his humor, of his sadness — of all expressions and manifestations of that which is alive in him. In thus giving of his life, he enriches the other person, he enhances the other's sense of aliveness by enhancing his own sense of aliveness. He does not give in order to receive; giving is in itself exquisite joy. But in giving he cannot help bringing something to life in the other person, and this which is brought to life reflects back to him.

Ψ

What most people in our culture mean by being lovable is essentially a mixture between being popular and having sex appeal.

Ψ

*Who will tell whether one happy moment of love
or the joy of breathing or walking on a bright
morning and smelling the fresh air, is not worth
all the suffering and effort which life implies.*

Ψ

Ivan Pavlov Quotes

Do not become a mere recorder of facts, but try and penetrate the mystery of their origin.

Ψ

Essentially only one thing in life interests us: our psychical constitution, the mechanism of which was and is wrapped in darkness. All human resources, art, religion, literature, philosophy and historical sciences, all of them join in bringing lights in this darkness. But man has still another powerful resource: natural science with its strictly objective methods. This science, as we all know, is making huge progress every day. The facts and considerations which I have placed before you at the end of my lecture are one out of numerous attempts to employ a consistent, purely scientific method of thinking in the study of the mechanism of the highest manifestations of life in the dog, the representative of the animal kingdom that is man's best friend.

Ψ

I am convinced that an important stage of human thought will have been reached when the physiological and the psychological, the objective and the subjective, are actually united, when the tormenting conflicts or contradictions between my consciousness and my body will have been factually resolved or discarded.

Ψ

I was, I am and will remain the Russian, the son of the Motherland. Her life first of all I will be interested in. I will live with her interests. With her's dignity I will strengthen mine.

Ψ

In gaining knowledge you must accustom yourself to the strictest sequence. You must be familiar with the very groundwork of science before you try to climb the heights. Never start on the "next" before you have mastered the "previous."

Ψ

In the dog two conditions were found to produce pathological disturbances by functional interference, namely, an unusually acute clashing of the excitatory and inhibitory processes, and the influence of strong and extraordinary stimuli. In man precisely similar conditions constitute the usual causes of nervous and psychic disturbances. Different conditions productive of extreme excitation, such as intense grief or bitter insults, often lead, when the natural reactions are inhibited by the necessary restraint, to profound and prolonged loss of balance in nervous and psychic activity.

Ψ

Learn the ABC of science before you try to ascend to its summit.

Ψ

Learn, compare, collect the facts!

Ψ

*Let the mind rise from victory to victory over
surrounding nature, let it but conquer for human
life and activity not only the surface of the earth
but also all that lies between the depth of the sea
and the outer limits of the atmosphere; let it
command for its service prodigious energy to flow
from one part of the universe to the other, let it
annihilate space for the transference of its
thoughts.*

Ψ

*Mankind will possess incalculable advantages
and extraordinary control over human
behavior when the scientific investigator will be
able to subject his fellow men to the same
external analysis he would employ for any
natural object, and when the human mind will
contemplate itself not from within but from
without.*

Ψ

*Modesty. Never think you know all. Though
others may flatter you, retain the courage to say,
"I am ignorant'*

Ψ

One can truly say that the irresistible progress of natural science since the time of Galileo has made its first halt before the study of the higher parts of the brain, the organ of the most complicated relations of the animal to the external world. And it seems, and not without reason, that now is the really critical moment for natural science; for the brain, in its highest complexity—the human brain—which created and creates natural science, itself becomes the object of this science.

Ψ

One can truly say that the irresistible progress of natural science since the time of Galileo has made its first halt before the study of the higher parts of the brain, the organ of the most complicated relations of the animal to the external world. And it seems, and not without reason, that now is the really critical moment for natural science; for the brain, in its highest complexity—the human brain—which created and creates natural science, itself becomes the object of this science.

Ψ

Only science, exact science about human nature itself, and the most sincere approach to it by the aid of the omnipotent scientific method, will deliver man from his present gloom and will purge him from his contemporary share in the sphere of interhuman relations.

Ψ

Perfect as the wing of a bird may be, it will never enable the bird to fly if unsupported by the air. Facts are the air of science. Without them a man of science can never rise. Without them your theories are vain surmises. But while you are studying, observing, experimenting, do not remain content with the surface of things. Do not become a mere recorder of facts, but try to penetrate the mystery of their origin. Seek obstinately for the laws that govern them.

Ψ

Science demands from a man all his life. If you had two lives that would not be enough for you. Be passionate in your work and in your searching.

Ψ

Science must be your passion. Remember that science claims a man's whole life. Had he two lives they would not suffice. Science demands an undivided allegiance from its followers. In your work and in your research there must always be passion.

Ψ

The digestive canal is in its task a complete chemical factory. The raw material passes through a long series of institutions in which it is subjected to certain mechanical and, mainly, chemical processing, and then, through innumerable side-streets, it is brought into the depot of the body. Aside from this basic series of institutions, along which the raw material moves, there is a series of lateral chemical manufactories, which prepare certain reagents for the appropriate processing of the raw material.

Ψ

The nervous system is the most complex and delicate instrument on our planet, by means of which relations, connections are established between the numerous parts of the organism, as well as between the organism, as a highly complex system, and the innumerable, external influences. If the closing and opening of electric current is now regarded as an ordinary technical device, why should there be any objection to the idea that the same principle acts in this wonderful instrument? On this basis the constant connection between the external agent and the response of the organism, which it evokes, can be rightly called an unconditioned reflex, and the temporary connection—a conditioned reflex.

Ψ

The Sun-Paul must consider only one thing: what is the relation of this or that external reaction of the animal to the phenomena of the external world?

Ψ

We must painfully acknowledge that, precisely because of its great intellectual developments, the best of man's domesticated animals—the dog— most often becomes the victim of physiological experiments. Only dire necessity can lead one to experiment on cats—on such impatient, loud, malicious animals. During chronic experiments, when the animal, having recovered from its operation, is under lengthy observation, the dog is irreplaceable; moreover, it is extremely touching. It is almost a participant in the experiments conducted upon it, greatly facilitating the success of the research by its understanding and compliance.

Ψ

Last Words

I am happy that this book reaches every reader around the world. I have included in it all those thoughts, reflections and words of the great ones that impressed and inspired me. I hope you found something useful and inspiring, too. Thank you for being a part of the wonderful world of this wonderful science, namely psychology. See you soon! Best regards, Valentin Boyadzhiev.